IT'S OFFICIAL!
YOU FUCKING HATE YOUR JOB!

BUT DON'T WORRY NOW YOU HAVE AN OUTLET FOR YOUR ANGER

INSIDE THIS BOOK YOU WILL FIND 20 MANDALAS FOR YOU TO SIT BACK AND COLOR

EACH ONE CONTAINS A QUOTE THAT YOU SHOULD DEFINITELY BE ABLE TO RELATE TO!

HAPPY COLORING

COLORING CREW

COLORING CREW

COLORING CREW

COLORING CREW

COLORING CREW

COLORING CREW

COLORING CREW

COLORING CREW

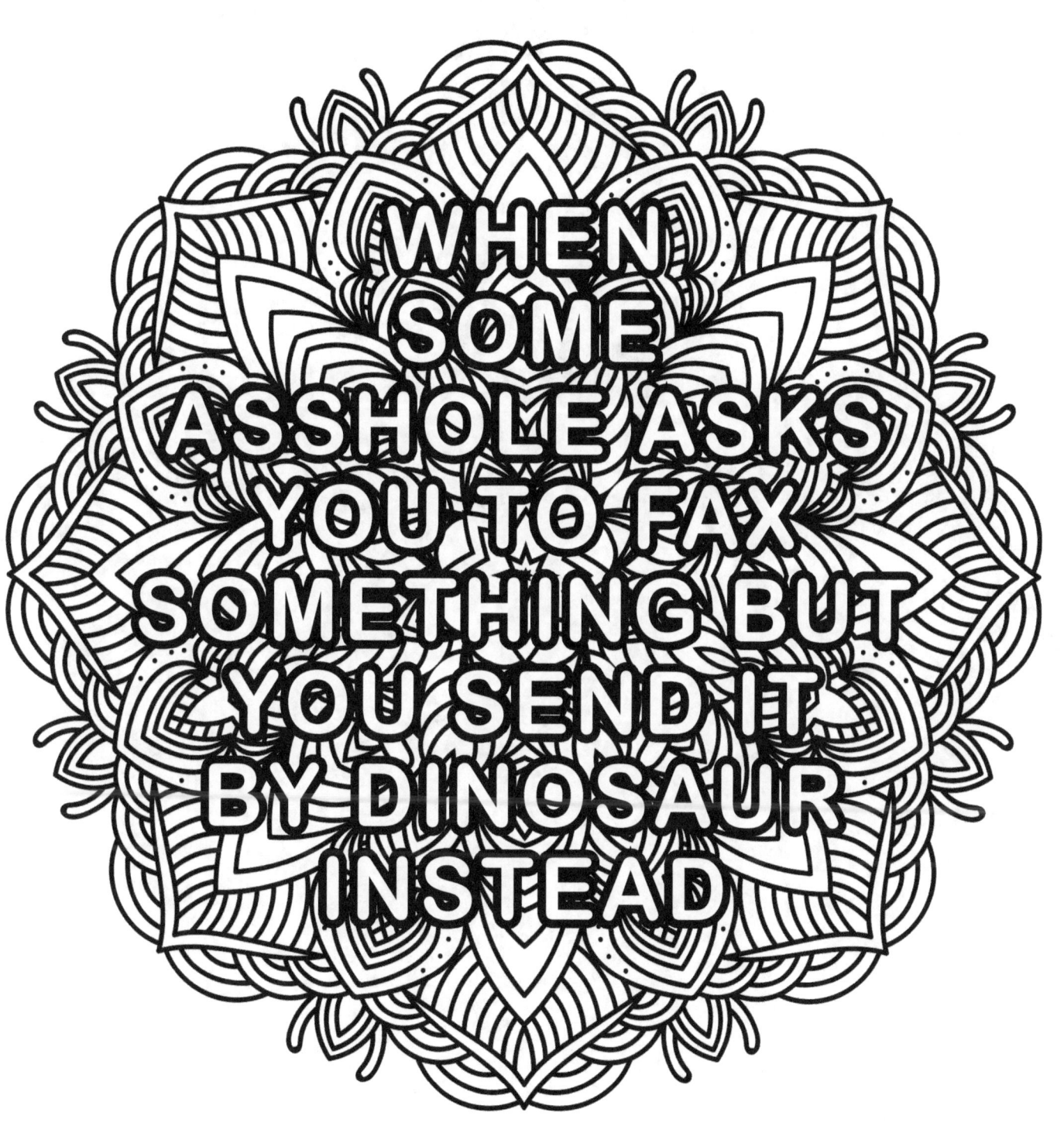

COLORING
CREW

COLORING CREW

COLORING CREW

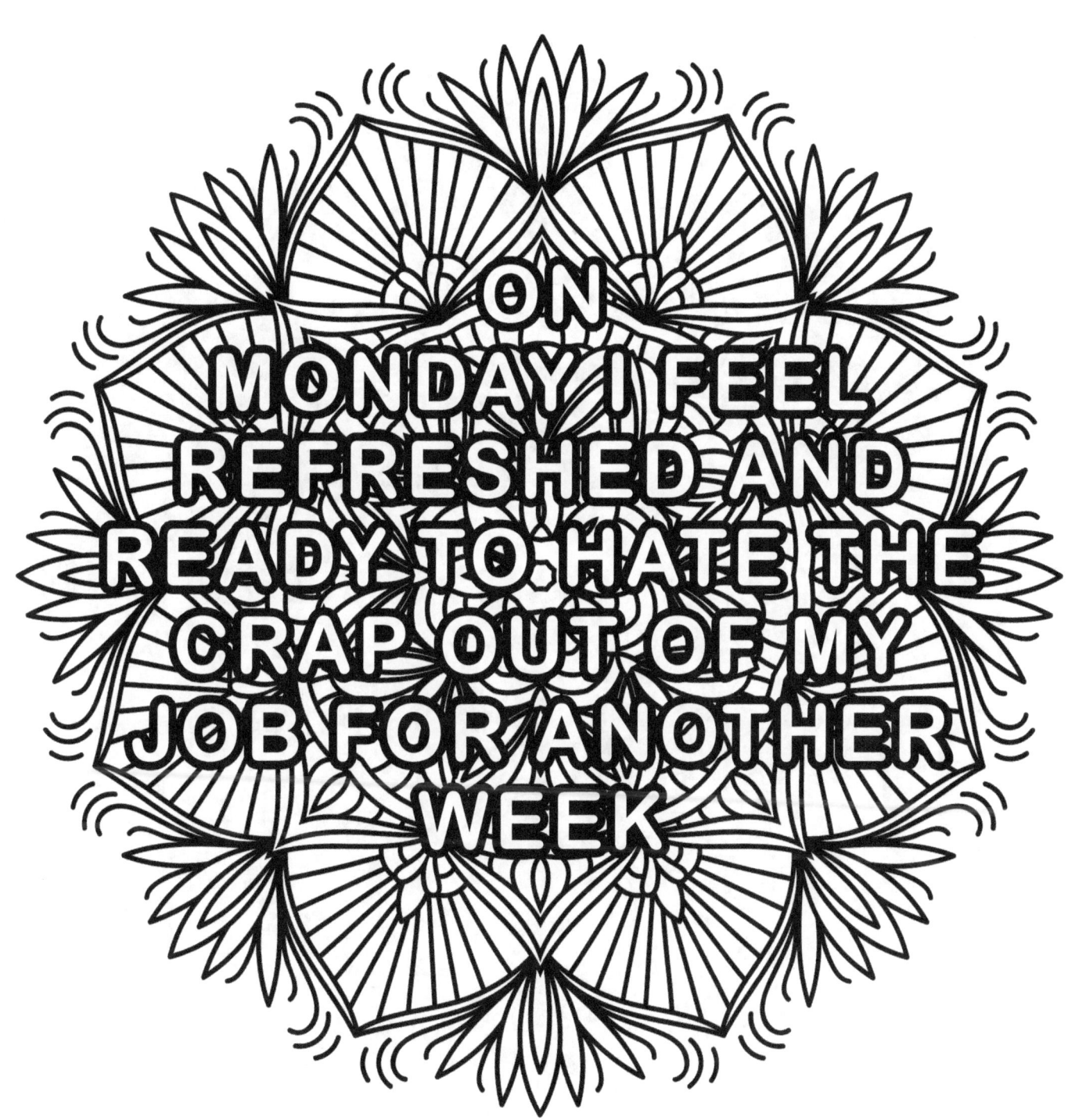

COLORING CREW

COLORING CREW

COLORING CREW

THANKS!
WE HOPE YOU HAD FUN!

IF YOU LIKED THIS BOOK THEN YOU YOU CAN
VIEW OUR FULL RANGE OF HILARIOUS ADULT
COLORING BOOKS BY GOING TO AMAZON AND
SEARCHING FOR "COLORING CREW" AND THEN
CLICKING ON OUR AUTHOR PAGE.

THANKS AGAIN!

COLORING CREW